WHAT IS A

Folktale?

GEOFF BARKER

Britannica®
Educational Publishing

IN ASSOCIATION WITH

ROSEN
EDUCATIONAL SERVICES

Published in 2014 by Britannica Educational Publishing (a trademark of Encyclopædia Britannica, Inc.) in association with The Rosen Publishing Group, Inc.
29 East 21st Street, New York, NY 10010

Distributed exclusively by Rosen Publishing.
To see additional Britannica Educational Publishing titles, go to rosenpublishing.com

First Edition

Britannica Educational Publishing
J.E. Luebering: Director, Core Reference Group
Anthony L. Green: Editor, Compton's by Britannica

Rosen Publishing
Hope Lourie Killcoyne: Executive Editor
Nelson Sá: Art Director

Library of Congress Cataloging-in-Publication Data

Barker, Geoff, 1963-
What is a Folktale?/Geoff Barker.—First Edition.
        pages cm.—(The Britannica Common Core Library)
Includes bibliographical references and index.
ISBN 978-1-62275-210-2 (library binding)—ISBN 978-1-62275-213-3 (pbk.)—ISBN 978-1-62275-214-0 (6-pack)
1. Tales—Juvenile literature. 2. Folk literature—History and criticism. I. Title.
GR74.B37 2014
398.2—dc23

2013022572

Manufactured in the United States of America.

Photo credits
Cover: Shutterstock: Photosani bg, Atelier Sommerland fg. Inside: Dreamstime: Kennytong 28, Outsiderzone 7, Ppart 20–21; Shutterstock: Joingate 18, Eric Isselee 23, Kavram 11, Patryk Kosmider 9, KUCO 14–15, LeshaBu 22, Leyn 13, John Lock 4, Melis 16, Molodec 5, Photosani 1bg, Rawcaptured 8, Showice 12, 24–25, Irina Solatges 6, Atelier Sommerland 1fg, 17, Theeraphon 19, Tukkki 26–27.

What Is a Folktale?	4
Why Are Folktales Told?	6
Themes in Folktales	8
Folktales Retold	10
The Giant Witch	10
Li Chi and the Serpent	12
Let's Compare	14
The Girl Who Lived with the Wolves	16
A Story and a Song	18
Let's Compare	20
The Warrior and the Owl	22
Selekana	24
Let's Compare	26
Write Your Own Folktale	28
Glossary	30
For More Information	31
Index	32

What Is a Folktale?

Folktales are made-up stories. Some are strange, some are happy, and others are sad. Folktales are told around the world, from Europe to China, and from Alaska to South America.

Folktales have been passed down by word of mouth. One person told a tale first, then the story spread. Soon whole families and communities knew and loved the tale.

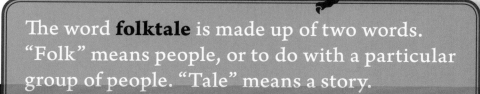

The word **folktale** is made up of two words. "Folk" means people, or to do with a particular group of people. "Tale" means a story.

Folktales changed as they were told. Eventually, they were written down. Today, there are different versions of the same folktale.

Some of the best folktales are scary!

Why Are Folktales Told?

Long ago, grandparents and parents told children folktales to teach them about their people's culture and history. Folktales were also used to teach children how best to live their lives. Folktales were powerful stories, so children remembered them and passed them on to their own children.

Australian Aboriginals have folktales known as the "Dreamtime." They are about the creation of all things.

Characters in folktales often have the same fears that people have in real life. Folktales were told to show people that they could face their fears, like the characters in the folktale. In many folktales, people use their wits to survive. Some folktales teach a moral, or a lesson. Some are just great stories, told for fun.

Most Native American folktales have a moral.

A **moral** is a lesson in how to behave well.

Themes in Folktales

If you read a lot of folktales, you will see similar types of stories. Some folktales are about how people cope with problems. Other stories look at how people behave. The characters may make right decisions or they may make wrong decisions.

Some folktales make you think about decisions.
Is it better to fight or is it wiser to run away?

The stories show how the characters live with their choices.

Folktales look at what makes people "good," such as kindness and bravery. They also explore what makes people "bad." Some stories look at what it is to be cowardly, mean, and selfish.

One African folktale explains how zebras got their stripes.

Folktales Retold

Now that we know what folktales are and why they are told, let's read and compare some of the world's most wonderful folktales.

The Giant Witch

This folktale comes from the Snohomish Native Americans.

A witch lived in the forest. When she was hungry, she visited the nearby village, gathering up children in her basket. One day, one of the children she took was a hunchbacked boy. She went home with the boy in a basket on her back. Grabbing onto a tree, the boy escaped. From the tree, he watched the witch.

Compare means to look at two or more things to see how alike or different they are.
The **Snohomish** come from the area north of Seattle in Washington.

He saw her light a fire, before placing the children on rocks near the fire. Then, she roasted and ate the children.

The boy went home and told everyone what he had seen. When the witch returned, she caught all the village girls. In the basket, the girls hatched a plan. The witch made a fire, then put the girls on the rocks. But before she could eat them, the girls worked together and pushed the witch into the fire.

Folktales are a very important part of Native American beliefs and culture.

Li Chi and the Serpent
This folktale comes from China.

A giant serpent lived in Fukien, in China. Every year, it ate a 12-year-old girl. One year, a brave girl named Li Chi offered herself for the snake. Her parents refused to let her go, but Li Chi left in secret. She took a sword and a hunting dog for protection, and some rice balls to tempt the snake from its cave.

A **serpent** is a snake.

Li Chi used her rice balls to trick the serpent that lived in the cave.

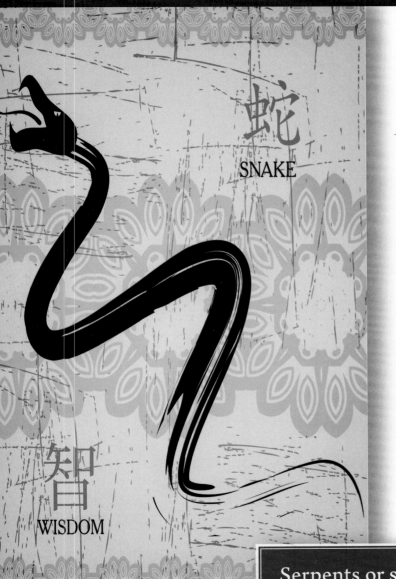

蛇
SNAKE

智
WISDOM

Li Chi headed for the serpent's cave, and placed the rice balls at its entrance. The snake smelled the rice balls. When he opened his mouth, the hunting dog bit him and Li Chi slashed him with her sword. Li Chi killed the giant serpent. When she returned home, the king made Li Chi his queen.

Serpents or snakes are found in many different Chinese folktales.

Let's Compare

Both *The Giant Witch* and *Li Chi and the Serpent* are tales about the bravery of children.

Li Chi stands up to the giant serpent. She is both fearless and smart. This folktale also shows how individuals can help their whole community.

STORYTELLERS

American writer Jane Yolen has collected over 150 wonderful fables in her book *Favorite Folktales from Around the World.*

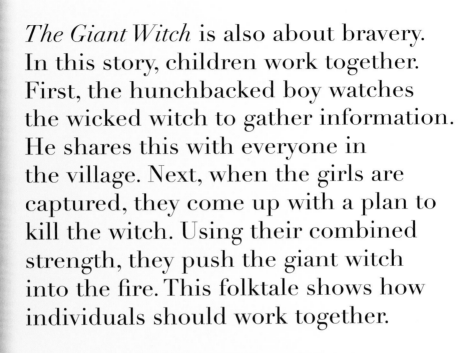

The Giant Witch is also about bravery. In this story, children work together. First, the hunchbacked boy watches the wicked witch to gather information. He shares this with everyone in the village. Next, when the girls are captured, they come up with a plan to kill the witch. Using their combined strength, they push the giant witch into the fire. This folktale shows how individuals should work together.

In the German folktale Hansel and Gretel, brave children also push a wicked witch into the fire.

The Girl Who Lived with the Wolves

This is a **Sioux** folktale from North America.

A girl's tribe was moving from winter to summer camp. The girl went to gather fruit, but got lost. Days later, she found the camp deserted. A wolf saw her and she was afraid. The wolf felt sorry for her and took the girl to live with his wolf pack. Soon she started to understand the wolves.

The **Sioux** are a Native American tribe who originally lived in what is now Minnesota.

In folktales, wolves are often something to fear.

The next spring, the girl saw some Sioux setting up camp. She was pleased to find them and left the wolves to be with the Sioux. The girl explained to them that the wolves hunted together and shared responsibilities. The chief told the tribe that they could learn from the wolves. If children, elders, or widows could not hunt, others should share their food with them.

The Sioux folktale has a strong message of working together.

A Story and a Song

This Indian folktale tells how a woman knew a story and a song, but kept them inside her.

The story and song were so sad that the woman did not sing the song or tell anyone the story. When she was asleep, the story and the song escaped. The story turned into a pair of shoes. The song became a man's coat.

The woman's husband came home. He found the shoes and coat, but his wife could not explain why they were there. The man was upset and went to the Monkey god's temple.

Many Indian paintings show the popular Monkey god.

In the temple, the man heard the lamps talking to each other. He heard how a woman had a story and a song, but would not share them with anyone, so they turned into shoes and a coat. He realized the lamps were talking about his wife.

He went home and asked his wife about the story and song. "What story? What song?" she asked.

Let's Compare

The Girl Who Lived with the Wolves and *A Story and a Song* seem different, but they are both about sharing.

The Sioux folktale shows how the whole tribe learns to share. Sharing was a very important part of the Sioux's way of life.

Native Americans of the Lakota Nation are better known as the Sioux.

The story from India tells the strange tale of a woman who misses the chance to share. She can share both her song and her story, but she chooses not to. The surprise ending shows what might happen if you do not share—even a song or a story. Sadly, you may not even realize what you have missed. This Indian folktale shows how important it is to be generous. You can bring joy by singing and passing on your stories.

> **Generous** means to give freely.

The Warrior and the Owl

This Tlingit story is about a warrior and his family who were starving. It comes from Alaska.

At night, alone, a warrior's wife used magic to catch fish to eat.

One night, the warrior's mother caught the wife. She told her son what was happening. The next night, the warrior watched his wife. He remembered her spell and used it to catch fish. He shared the fish with his mother. His wife woke up and saw them eating. She realized that they knew her secret.

Tlingit people came from southeastern Alaska.

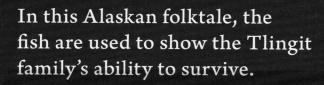

In this Alaskan folktale, the fish are used to show the Tlingit family's ability to survive.

The wife ran away. She lost her magical powers and became smaller. Feathers sprouted from her arms and face. The warrior reached his wife and saw that she was an owl. She hooted and flew off. The warrior was sad. He only wanted to show his wife how to be generous. Today, the cry of the owl hooting reminds people of the wife's selfishness.

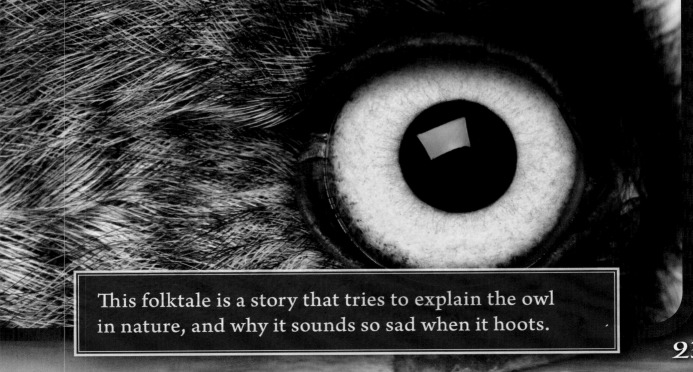

This folktale is a story that tries to explain the owl in nature, and why it sounds so sad when it hoots.

Selekana

This story comes from Botswana.

Girls were jealous of Selekana's beauty. They fooled her into throwing her jewelry into a pool for the river god. Selekana stood by the pool and cried out, "Show me my beads!"

The pool opened and Selekana found herself in a cave. She saw an old woman with one arm and one leg. Selekana felt sorry for the woman and did her chores. The woman rewarded Selekana by giving her jewelry and clothes.

Botswana is a country in southern Africa.

She helped Selekana escape from a cannibal that lived in the cave, and showed her how to leave the pool.

Selekana told the girls how she got her new jewelry. They went to the pool and met the old woman. They laughed at her and refused to help her. The old woman threatened to leave them with the cannibal. Afraid, they promised never to be selfish or jealous again. The woman helped them to escape. The girls realized how bad their behaviour was, and they became kind, unselfish women.

There are many different versions of this African folktale, but most include beads and jewelry.

Let's Compare

The Warrior and the Owl and *Selekana* are about selfishness.

In the Alaskan folktale, the warrior's young wife is selfish. She is discovered by both her mother-in-law and husband, and loses her magical powers. The story ends unhappily, as the wife turns into an owl. This folktale also tries to explain why an owl's hooting sounds so sad.

Animals were very important to Native American culture, and many are shown in drawings and carvings.

The girls who are jealous of Selekana trick her. When they hear of the riches she has gained, they are interested only in how they can also get jewelry from the old woman. Unlike Selekana, they felt nothing for the old woman, and they did not want to help her. However, unlike the wife in the Alaskan tale, they are given the chance to change their mean and selfish ways.

Write Your Own Folktale

A re you ready to write your own folktale? Here are some simple steps to help you start:

1. Pick your setting: Think about where you want to set your folktale. For example, will it be in a dark, damp cave or high on a cliff top?

If you want to write a Native-American style folktale, why not base your characters on the animals and creatures on a totem pole?

2. Choose characters: Decide who your characters will be. They may be people or creatures. How might they behave? Are they good or bad?

3. Create a turning point: Many folktales have a turning point, such as discovering that someone acted wrongly. What will your folktale include?

4. Research your folktale: Find out details about your theme so you can use them in your folktale.

5. Sketch your folktale: Make a "map" of your folktale. Give it a beginning, middle, and end.

6. Write and rewrite! Write your tale, then read it through. Change anything you do not like.

Finished? Read your folktale to a friend, or one of your family members. Send it in an e-mail to your teacher or a member of your family. You could even post it onto your family's website or blog.

GLOSSARY

Aboriginals The first people to live in a region or area. Australian Aboriginals were the first people to live in Australia.

bravery Not being afraid of things and showing courage.

cannibal Someone who eats human flesh.

characters The people or animals in a story.

chief The head of a tribe.

communities Groups of people living together in one place.

cowardly Showing shameful fear.

culture The customs and traditions of a group of people.

decisions Choices, things you decide.

elders The older people in a tribe.

history Things that happened in the past.

hunchbacked Having a bent or hunched-over back.

responsibilities Duties.

selfish To think only of oneself and of no one else.

setting Where a story takes place.

starving To be very hungry.

temple A place where people go to worship.

theme An idea found in a story.

threatened Warned.

tribe A group of people who are related and who share a culture.

turning point Something that happens to change the course of things.

versions Different stories about the same thing, but with different details.

wits Brains, smart thinking.

Books

Cleveland, Rob. *The Drum: A Folktale from India* (Welcome to Story Cove). Atlanta, GA: August House, 2006.

Conger, David and Kay Lyons, Liana Romulo, Joan Suyenaga, and Marian Davies Toth. *Asian Children's Favorite Stories: A Treasury of Folktales from China, Japan, Korea, India, the Philippines, Thailand, Indonesia and Malaysia*. North Clarendon, VT: Tuttle Publishing, 2006.

Garland, Sherry. *Children of the Dragon: Selected Tales from Vietnam*. Gretna, LA: Pelican Publishing, 2012.

Krensky, Stephen. *How Coyote Stole the Summer: A Native American Folktale* (On My Own Folklore). Minneapolis, MN: Millbrook Press, 2009.

So-Un, Kim. *Korean Children's Favorite Stories*. North Clarendon, VT: Tuttle Publishing, 2004.

Websites

Due to the changing nature of Internet links, Rosen Publishing has developed an online list of Websites related to the subject of this book. This site is updated regularly. Please use this link to access the list:

http://www.rosenlinks.com/corel/folk

INDEX

Aboriginals 6
Africa 9, 24, 25
Alaska 4, 22, 26, 27
animals 26, 28
Australia 6

Botswana 24
boy 10, 11, 15
bravery 9, 12, 14, 15

cannibal 25
cave 12, 13, 24, 25, 28
characters 7, 8, 9, 28, 29
children 6, 10, 11, 14, 15, 17
China 4, 12
communities 4, 14
creation 6

decisions 8
Dreamtime 6

fears 7, 14, 16
fight 8
fire 11, 15
fish 22
Fukien 12

girls 11, 12–13, 15, 16–17, 20, 24–25, 27

India 18, 19, 21

jewelry 24, 25, 27

magic 22, 23, 26
Monkey god 18, 19
moral 7

Native American 7, 10, 11, 16, 20, 26, 28

owl 22–23, 26

rice balls 12, 13
river god 24

Seattle 10
selfish 9, 23, 25, 26, 27
serpent 12–13, 14
setting 28
share 15, 17, 19, 20, 21, 22
shoes 18, 19
Sioux 16, 17, 20
snake 12, 13
Snohomish people 10
song 18–19, 20, 21
sword 12, 13

themes 8–9, 29
Tlingit 22
totem pole 28
tribe 16, 17, 20

warrior 22–23, 26
witch 10–11, 14, 15
wolves 16–17, 20

zebras 9